I0617368

Environmental Lifestyle Guide

For Grade 10 Students

VOL.4 OF 11

Health & Beauty

Jahangir Asadi

Vancouver, BC CANADA

Published by: Silosa Consulting Group Inc.
Vancouver, BC **CANADA**
Email: Info@Silosa.ca
www.silosa.ca

Ordering Information:
Quantity sales. Special discounts are available on quantity purchases by universities, schools, corporations, associations, and others. For details, contact the "Sales Department" at the above mentioned email address.

Environmental lifestyle Guide Vol.4 for Grade.10/J.Asadi —1st ed.
ISBN: 978-1-990451-78-2

Contents

We hope that, 10,000 years from now, future generations will be able to see flowers that provide bees with nectar and pollen and...
BEES provide flowers with the means to reproduce by spreading pollen from flower to flower,....

Jahangir Asadi

This book is dedicated to my professor, Dr.Bijan Esfandiari

Introduction

This book is part of an eleven volume series that is meant to be a standard text-book series, for grades 9 to 12. TTAIN & ESFK & SCG improves quality of life and reduces environmental degradation by fostering new consumption patterns and sustainable lifestyles through International Cooperative Extension Service programs at houses, offices, schools and libraries all over the globe.

Climate change is real. Therefore people have the potential to make a difference now and for future generations. This book provides climate science basics, including the roles that lifestyles and populations play in the climate scenario, the significance of carbon footprints, and an overview of the current climate situation. The manual has been categorized based on humanity's needs starting first with food and ending with tourism. The manual then illustrates the difference between adaptation (taking steps to live with the changes) and mitigation (taking steps to slow the rate of change.)

Adaptation examples include food, energy, transportation, recreation. Mitigation focuses on effectively engaging with local governments, through serving on advisory boards, communicating with public officials, educational institutes, schools, universities, libraries and leading communities towards climate change actions.

One useful way to mitigate climate change is through increasing public knowledge to better understand the impact of the rate of change on plants and animals. This is crucial for preserving species; and for assessing potential insects and disease outbreaks in agriculture, natural resources and public health.

Taking personal action is a key element of this manual.

Citizens are challenged to consume 20% fewer resources, to bring world consumption levels down as much as possible. Readers are given 12 practical steps to take to make the changes. The resources section provides additional information, and readers are encouraged to contact the author for further questions.

As an accessibility action, we have provided Online international courses on climate change control as well. You can access the courses via the following link:

http://TopTenAward.org

SILOSA Consulting Group (SCG)

Silosa Consulting Group (SCG) was established to provide outstanding consulting services of management system & educational standards to individuals, groups, companies, schools, and organizations all over the globe. SCG is publishing an "Environmental Lifestyle Guide " book series as a standard textbook related to increasing environmental awareness of students means being aware of the natural environment and making choices that benefit the earth, rather than hurt it. Vol.1 to 11 (for grades 9 to 12) providing some of the ways to practice environmental awareness include: **Recycling**, **Conserving energy and water**, **Reuse, Activism, and others**.

SCG book publishing services and distribution services are connected to over 39,000 booksellers worldwide, including Apple, Amazon, Barnes & Noble, Indigo, Google Play Books, and many more. SCG has enough experiences to help create new and effective environmental educational programmes in different countries all over the world. For more detail, visit our website : http://silosa.ca and/or send your enquirer to the following email:

info@silosa.ca

CHAPTER 1

About ISO 14000 for Students

The International Organization for Standardization is an independent, non-governmental organization, the members of which are the standards organizations of the 165 member countries. It is the world's largest developer of voluntary international standards and it facilitates world trade by providing common standards among nations. More than twenty thousand standards have been set, covering everything from manufactured products and technology to food safety, agriculture, and healthcare.

Kids ISO 14000s
"Kids ISO 14000s" is a new environmental education program for children, based on ISO 14000s, which is international standard for environmental management. Primary aims of this program are: -
1. To teach and train children how to manage the environmental issues (such as energy saving) by themselves through the working book and guide book of this program,
2. To certify those children who showed good accomplishment in the program from highly international authority (as is the case of ISO 14000s)
3. To network those children through the international network (Kids International Network), so that the children can work on the environment, internationally.

2. System of Kids ISO 14000s Program

The system of Kids ISO 14000s Program consists of

1. Operation Headquarter (ArTech).

2. Workbook, Guidebook (originally published by ArTech, and local versions are produced by each countries).

3. Eco-Kids-Instructors for local operation and evaluation of the performance of the children.

4. International accreditation committee for accreditation of accomplishment of the children, for certification of the Eco-Kids-Instructors, as well as overall checks of this program.

5. Linkage with international organizations (such as UNU, UNESCO, etc. …) And also national organizations

More information can be obtained :

www.ISO.org

Canada

Environmental Sustain for Future kids established in Vancouver, BC Canada in 2020. (ESFK) is an international ecolabel focused on taking care of environment for future of kids. ESFK defined as 'self-declared' environmental claims made by manufacturers and businesses based on ISO 14020 series of standards, the claimant can declare the environmental objectives and targets in relation to taking care of environment for future kids. However, this declaration will be verifiable.

Environmental Sustain for Future Kids
Vancouver, BC CANADA

Email: info@esfk.org
Web: www.esfk.org

STEP FOUR

All about 'Eco-friendly' Health
and Beauty Products

Health and beauty encompasses a variety of products, including fragrances, makeup, hair care and coloring products, sunscreen, toothpaste, and products for bathing, nail care, and shaving. The industry overlaps with other markets like chemical, health care, and petroleum.

In this book, Health and Beauty products divided into Three main catogries:

- Cosmetics
- Baby
- Hygine

Green Cosmetics:
The Push for Sustainable Beauty

As public interest in sustainability continues to climb, many cosmetic manufacturers are seeking more natural and environmentally-friendly emulsifiers and ingredients for their products. The benefits of "green" beauty products extend beyond trends — increasing studies show the toxicity of conventional cosmetics, and the natural cosmetics market continues to grow rapidly and consistently.

Manufacturing companies interested in venturing into the green market must know the details behind the sustainability movement, including the benefits of going green and the potential of the market. In modern marketing, the word "green" has become synonymous with "organic" or "healthy." When a consumer sees the phrase "green cosmetics," they will automatically make eco-friendly assumptions about the product or company.

But the field of green cosmetics still needs clarification. Typically, the term is used to describe products using environmentally-friendly formulations, production practices or packaging methods. In the United States, the Federal Trade Commission (FTC) has published guidelines to clarify what green or natural means in marketing terms, though these guidelines are still loosely defined.

With respect to the cosmetics industry, "green" and "sustainable" cosmetics are defined as cosmetic products using natural ingredients produced from renewable raw materials. Many companies use petrochemical ingredients derived from petrol, a non-renewable and economically volatile resource. Bio-based oleochemicals, on the other hand, derive from renewable plant and bacteria sources and are the crux of the green cosmetics movement.

How Are Sustainable Cosmetics Made?

Cosmetics developers worldwide are doggedly pursuing these oleochemicals, along with any potential sources for them. Some examples of common sources include:

Natural Oils: Palm and coconut oils are often used to derive fatty alcohols, which are used as chemical surfactants. Other oils include argan oil and avocado oil. Glycerine, a derivative of palm oil, is a common byproduct.

Agricultural Plants: Soybeans, corn and other agricultural plants are used throughout the cosmetic industry to produce oils and alcohols. Green cosmetic emulsifiers, surfactants and biocatalysts are derived using these plants, which can be cheaply and sustainably sourced.

Bacteria: One example of a renewable resource currently under development is the Deinococcus bacteria, a bacterium studied by Deinove in France for its chemical production properties. Deinove has used the bacterium to create aromatic ingredients and pigments for the cosmetic industry, representing a potential market value in the hundreds of millions of dollars.

Manufacturers split these raw materials into oleochemicals at a processing plant. The fats or oils are divided by hydrolysis, which uses water, or alcoholysis, which uses alcohol.

Ingredients That Aren't Sustainable

Avoid many of the toxic elements found in popular brands. These chemicals damage environmental and human health, and consumers should never read them on a "green" label.

Aluminum:

Commonly used in antiperspirants, aluminum enters the body through the underarm tissue and blocks sweat ducts. However, it has also been linked to breast cancer, Alzheimer's disease and osteoporosis.

Dibutyl phthalate (DBP):

Often found in nail products, DBP is a solvent for dyes. Considered toxic to human reproduction, it enhances the ability of other chemicals to cause genetic mutations. While Canada has banned DBP from all children's toys, no action has yet been taken against its presence in cosmetics.

Coal tar dyes:

On labels, coal tar dyes are listed as p-phenylenediamine or colors titled "CI" and followed by a five-digit number. These dyes are mixtures of petrochemicals, and they have been linked to cancer in humans.

BHA and BHT:

BHA and BHT are synthetic antioxidants used as preservatives, and they are most common in lipsticks and moisturizing creams. The European Commission has released evidence that BHA and BHT disrupt the endocrine system.

Formaldehyde-releasing preservatives:

These preservatives are present in a wide range of cosmetics, as well as in cleaning products such as toilet bowl cleaners. As their name suggests, formaldehyde-releasing preservatives continuously release small amounts of formaldehyde, a known human carcinogen.

Examples of Sustainable Cosmetics:

Many manufacturers have found success using oleochemical-based products, and beyond creating high-quality and effective products, they have gained a loyal customer following. Here are some of the most well-known, sustainable cosmetics companies and their products:

Native: Native produces deodorants with organic, natural ingredients. Native has built their brand around "simple, nontoxic ingredients you can understand." Their oleochemical-derived ingredients include shea butter, coconut oil and castor bean oil.

Burt's Bees: From simple beeswax candles to a lip-product empire, Burt's Bees has become an international leader in sustainability. The company creates cosmetics and personal care products, and in addition to natural, organic ingredients, it has a "no-waste" manufacturing policy. They rely on botanical oils, herbs and beeswax to come up with their world-recognized products.

RMS Beauty: RMS Beauty provides a wide range of cosmetics, from foundation to mascara. Dedicated to using organic ingredients, RMS creates non-toxic makeup products that heal and protect the skin. They use low-heat processing to ensure their ingredients remain as natural as possible.

Blissoma: Focusing on skincare, Blissoma offers a large selection of products organized by skin type and need. Their preservative-free cosmetics include natural ingredients like fruit enzymes, Vitamin C and organic herbs and grains.

Drunk Elephant: Committed to using clean, natural ingredients, Drunk Elephant manufactures a range of sustainable skin care products. They have a devoted consumer following and strive to create products that are both clinically-effective and naturally-sourced.

It's possible for any company to incorporate green materials in their cosmetics. If you want to branch into the world of sustainable, oleochemical-derived products, begin with some of these safe and effective ingredients.

Fatty Acids: Fatty acids like coconut fatty acid, stearic acid and oleic acid are green ingredients used as lubricants, adhesives and release agents, as well as emulsifiers and base stock. You can incorporate naturally derived fatty acids into a wide range of cosmetic products, including soaps, ceramic powders, lotions and creams.

Castor Oil: Made by pressing the seeds of the castor plant, castor oil is a beneficial ingredient that has a range of anti-inflammatory and pain-relieving properties. When used in hair cosmetics, materials like Jamaican Black Castor Oil both remove impurities and clarify the scalp, resulting in more effective and more eco-friendly product.

MCT Coconut Oil: Extracted from the kernel of mature coconuts, MCT Coconut oil is a highly specialized and versatile carrier oil. Light, smooth and easily absorbed into the skin, MCT oil is especially useful in skincare products. Because it doesn't leave an oily residue, MCT oil is ideal for products marketed as oil-free or for sensitive skin types.

DMDM Hydantoin: A powerful antimicrobial agent, DMDM Hydantoin is a halogen-free preservative. This eco-friendly ingredient can be added to both rinse-off and leave-on products, including eye and skin creams, shampoo and conditioner, sunscreen, liquid soap and make-up remover.

Phenoxyethanol: Inhibiting both bacteria and mold growth, phenoxyethanol is an effective preservative used in a wide range of green cosmetics, from lotions and creams to make-up and gels. Phenoxyethanol serves a variety of roles within cosmetics, including solvent, fixative and topical anesthetic functions.

Committed to sustainable manufacturing, Acme-Hardesty offers each of these green ingredients for manufacturers in the cosmetics industry.

Why Buy Natural and Sustainable Cosmetics

Environmental Responsibility

Modern consumers have a growing global consciousness, and they care about social and environmental responsibility. One of the main benefits of sustainable products is their kinder environmental impact.

Every week, new stories surface about dangerous carbon outputs or vast plastic floats in the ocean. Many petrochemicals in conventional cosmetics are toxic pollutants and degrade the environment as well as our bodies. As we become more ecologically aware, consumers demand natural, low-polluting products.

A recent example of pollution and consumer demand is the ban of microbeads. Microbeads are tiny pieces of plastic found in many shower scrubs and exfoliating products. However, they do not dissolve, and in 2015, a study reported that over eight trillion microbeads were being washed into our waterways every day. Later that year, U.S. President Barack Obama signed a bill banning the small plastics, illustrating that environmental stewardship is an increasing priority to the nation and its consumers.

Increased Effectiveness

Natural and oleochemical ingredients are less likely to cause skin irritation or allergic reactions. Without synthetic, toxic chemicals or artificial colors, sustainable products rely on the healing properties found naturally in plants and animals — the ingredients humans have been using for centuries. Consider glycerine, a natural derivative of palm oil. The clear, non-toxic liquid is used in soaps, pharmaceuticals and cosmetics. Since it is a humectant, glycerine can retain water, making it an excellent moisturizer. Glycerine enhances the body's hygroscopic characteristics, encouraging the skin to absorb and hold on to water. As a non-irritating substance, it can be applied anywhere on the body. It is an effective anti-aging ingredient and, due to its anti-microbial properties, can also serve as an acne treatment.

Long-Term Health

While petrochemicals may deliver short-term results, the long-term effects can be highly toxic to humans and the environment. Years of synthetic cosmetics use has been traced to headaches, eye damage, acne, hormonal imbalance and premature aging. Phthalates have even been linked to cancer and type II diabetes. By choosing sustainable cosmetics, a consumer forgoes the stress and uncertainty of toxic, synthetic products and invests in their long-term health and beauty.

Why Produce Green Cosmetics?

1. Improved Product Quality
High-quality cosmetics provide effective results without putting the consumer at risk. However, many petrochemical products, like mineral oil, present a low level of toxicity to users. When aerosolized and inhaled, such products have been shown to be allergens and, as some studies suggest, may cause cancer. With most bio-based products, the toxicity to the end-user is reduced, creating safer, higher-quality products.

2. Enhances Brand Reputation
Green products send a message to consumers — this company is committed to quality, safety and sustainability, and is worthy of your trust. As more and more people grow concerned about synthetic products, consumers are looking for companies that practice transparency and honesty. By moving towards sustainable, green products, you show your global and social awareness. This promotes customer loyalty to a brand, not just to products. People will begin — and continue — to purchase a company's products because they agree with its mission.

3. Increases Corporate Responsibility
Green cosmetics also present a unique opportunity for cosmetics manufacturers to focus on corporate responsibility. In addition to the positive impacts green marketing can have on a company's image, taking the extra steps of sustainable sourcing or packaging can also make a significant impact. When a company increases its sustainability initiatives, it takes ownership for its impact on global health and economies. By taking corporate responsibility for its manufacturing, a business gains authority and respect among consumers as well as suppliers and other members of the distribution chain.

The Future of Sustainable Cosmetics

Manufacturers shifting to sustainable cosmetics production have a promising future. The growing interest in sustainable cosmetics has had a significant effect on the cosmetics market. With an increasing number of consumers and retailers demanding cosmetics with natural or sustainable ingredients, the green cosmetics market has experienced a 15 percent annual growth rate.

This growth rate far outpaces that global personal care and cosmetics industry, which is currently sustaining an overall 5 percent annual growth rate. By 2025, the organic beauty market will reach $25.11 billion. Within the personal care industry, the oleochemicals market is increasing as cosmetic manufacturers continue to turn away from petrochemicals. Fatty acids, in particular, should experience boosts on the green side of the market, considering that they accounted for 57 percent of the total oleochemical product demand in 2013.

The Asia-Pacific region is an area of particular interest for this market since the region accounted for 41.9 percent of the total oleochemicals market in 2013 for its abundance of raw materials and large consumer base. Both figures are unsurprising considering the quantities of bulk cosmetic glycerine regularly exported from the region. As petrochemicals continue to experience volatility in the market, turning to sustainable material sources may be the best long-term decision for cosmetics manufacturers worldwide.

Consumers are increasingly demanding sustainable products that are not toxic to themselves or the environment. The natural market is growing exponentially, and choosing raw, natural materials will cement your brand as a safe choice — both environmentally and economically.

EU and UK Cosmetic product definition:

Based on the definition of the cosmetic products, products that may seem to be cosmetics, like nail wraps, a comb or a toothbrush, therefore aren't cosmetics, even though they are placed in contact with the external parts of the human body, and their primary function is to change appearance, but they wouldn't be considered a substance or a mixture.

A cosmetic product in Europe and UK is defined in the Regulation 1223/2009 as follows:

'cosmetic product' means any substance or mixture intended to be placed in contact with the external parts of the human body (epidermis, hair system, nails, lips and external genital organs) or with the teeth and the mucous membranes of the oral cavity with a view exclusively or mainly to cleaning them, perfuming them, changing their appearance, protecting them, keeping them in good condition or correcting body odours. (EU Regulation 1223/2009, Article 2.1.a)

Since products have to be placed in contact with the external parts of the human body or with the teeth and the mucous membranes of the oral cavity, any product intended to be ingested, inhaled, injected or implanted into the human body would also not be considered a cosmetic product in the EU or the UK. Breast implants then aren't cosmetics, even though their primary function is also to change appearance.

The product has to be a:

CLASSES OF COSMETIC PRODUCTS:

Cosmetic product may include:

creams, emulsions, lotions, gels and oils for the skin,
face masks,
tinted bases (liquids, pastes, powders),
make-up powders,
after-bath powders,
hygienic powders,
toilet soaps,
deodorant soaps,
perfumes, toilet waters and eau de Cologne,
bath and shower preparations (salts, foams, oils, gels),
depilatories,
deodorants and antiperspirants,
hair colorants,
products for waving, straightening and fixing hair,
hair-setting products,
hair-cleansing products (lotions, powders, shampoos),
hair-conditioning products (lotions, creams, oils),
hairdressing products (lotions, lacquers, brilliantines),
shaving products (creams, foams, lotions),
make-up and products removing make-up,
products intended for application to the lips,
products for care of the teeth and the mouth,
products for nail care and make-up,
products for external intimate hygiene,
sunbathing products,
products for tanning without sun,
skin-whitening products,
anti-wrinkle products

The Cosmetic Product has to be intended to place in contact with:

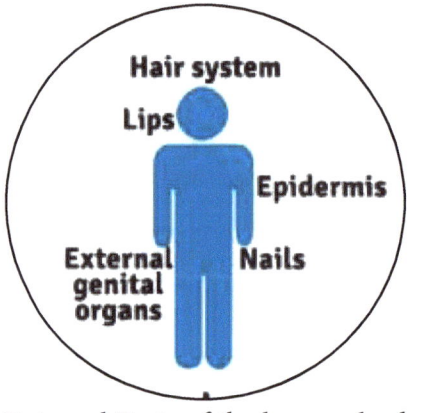

External Parts of the human body

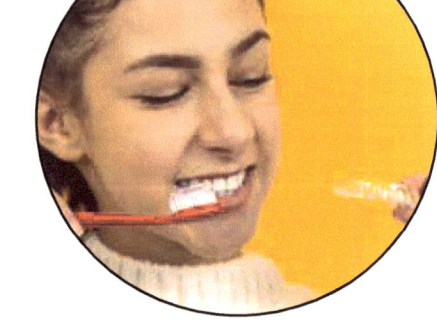

Teeth

Mucous membranes of the oral cavity

The assessment of whether a product is a ECO friendly cosmetic product has to be made on the basis of a case-by-case assessment, taking into account all characteristics of the products.

The purpose of cosmetic product has to be exclusively or mainly:

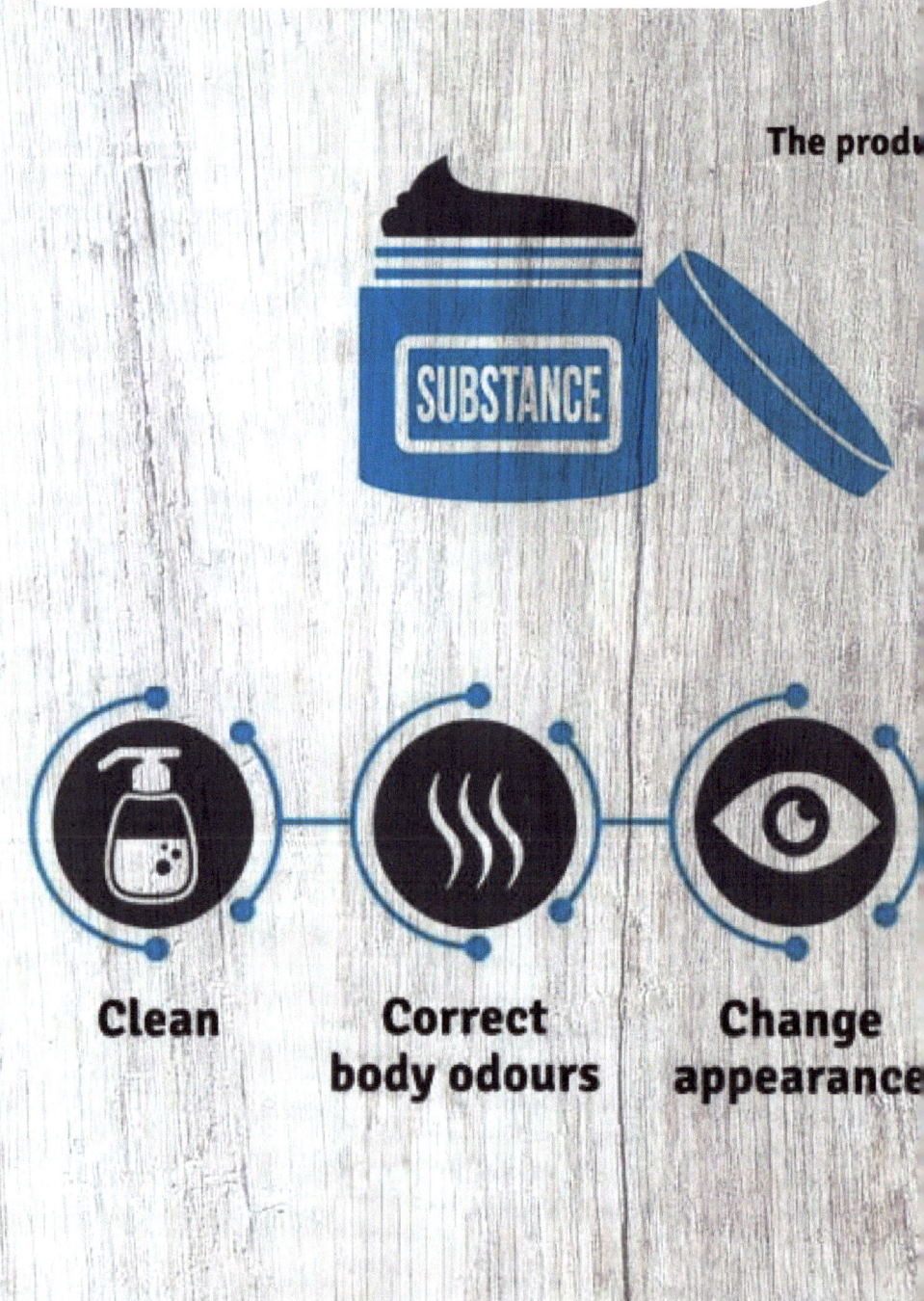

The prod

SUBSTANCE

Clean

Correct body odours

Change appearance

s to be a:

MIXTURE

Protect

Keep in good condition

Perfume

Cosmetics FAQs:
What is meant by vegan cosmetics?
When a beauty product is marked as vegan, it means the same thing a vegan diet does. This label infers that the product does not contain any animal or its byproducts in it.

What is the difference between vegan makeup and regular makeup?
Most often, the difference between vegan and vegetarian cosmetics is that products labeled "vegetarian" will contain natural animal-made ingredients, most commonly beeswax and honey, which are avoided by vegans. Many green beauty brands that aren't 100% vegan will state that they're vegetarian. … Testing Ingredients.

What is cruelty free in cosmetics?
Cruelty-free cosmetics is a category containing all cosmetics that have not been tested on animals. … Many companies brand themselves as cruelty-free but still use raw materials that have been tested on animals.

"Cruelty-free" can be used to imply that:

- Neither the product nor its ingredients have ever been tested on animals. This is highly unlikely however, as almost all ingredients in use today have been tested on animals somewhere, at some time, by someone — and could be tested again.
- While the ingredients have been tested on animals, the final product has not.
- The manufacturer itself did not conduct animal tests but instead relied on a supplier to test for them — or relied on another company's previous animal-test results.
- Either the ingredients or the product have not been tested on animals within the last five, ten, or twenty years (but perhaps were before, and could be again).
- As in the case of the CCIC's Leaping Bunny Program, neither the ingredients nor the products have been tested on animals after a certification date and will not be tested on animals in the future.

Can skin care products cause allergic reaction?

Personal care products like makeup, skin cream, and fragrances also commonly cause rashes. It's not well understood how chemical compounds in personal care products trigger these rashes, called allergic contact dermatitis.

Can you suddenly become allergic to something?

Allergies can develop at any point in a person's life. Usually, allergies first appear early in life and become a lifelong issue. However, allergies can start unexpectedly as an adult. A family history of allergies puts you at a higher risk of developing allergies some time in your life.

How to Prevent Cosmetic Allergies?

Avoid ingredients in cosmetics and skincare products that are irritating to your skin. Look for labels such as "hypoallergenic", "sensitivity tested", "paraben-free", "phthalate-free", "non-comedogenic" and "fragrance-free".

What is a Non-GMO?

Non-GMO means a product was produced without genetic engineering and its ingredients are not derived from GMOs.

What is Paraben free?

Parabens can act like the hormone estrogen in the body and disrupt the normal function of hormone systems affecting male and female reproductive system functioning, reproductive development, fertility and birth outcomes. While nearly all beauty products use some kind of preservatives to make their products last longer, paraben-free cosmetics may be safer to use. The term "paraben-free" is meant to let consumers know that these harmful chemicals aren't a part of the product formula.

What is SLS ?

Sodium Lauryl Sulfate (SLS) strips the skin of its natural oils which causes dry skin, irritation and allergic reactions. It can also be very irritating to the eyes. Inflammatory skin reactions include itchy skin and scalp, eczema and dermatitis.

The Most Common Allergens in Health & Beauty Products;

Fragrance
Fragrance is one of the most common causes of allergic contact dermatitis in skincare products. "Fragrance can contain hundreds of components, and companies are not required to disclose all the ingredients that make up what's labeled as 'fragrance,'" he says. Fragrance-free is also not the same as unscented (unscented products might contain masking fragrances that neutralize perfume). Between the two, "fragrance-free is the better option if you have sensitive skin."

Parabens
"Parabens are a group of synthetic compounds commonly used as preservatives in a wide range of personal care products," . "They might cause an allergic reaction in certain people, and are more likely to irritate those with existing skin issues like eczema, psoriasis, and contact dermatitis."

Sulfates
Sodium laureth sulfate and sodium lauryl sulfate are two common skincare, bath, and hair product ingredients that also may cause rashes and itching.

Dyes
Dyes—most often found in hair products and more pigmented cosmetics—are another culprit; The dye ingredient which most often causes allergic reactions is paraphenylenediamine (PPD).

Benzyl Alcohol
"Benzyl alcohol is used for its fragrance, preservative abilities, and antimicrobial action, "In rare cases, it can cause a hive-like reaction."

Propylene Glycol
Propylene glycol is often used in moisturizers as a humectant to lock in moisture—and even at low concentrations, allergic reactions can occur, he warns.

Essential Oils

Last but not least? Essential oils. "They're highly concentrated substances that are extracted from various trees and plants for their fragrance and antimicrobial action," Tea tree oil is the most common essential oil allergen. Steer clear of products containing essential oils if your skin tends to be sensitive.

Today's sustainable paper eco friendly cosmetic packaging offers a perfect material for products that can be reduced and reused, are 100% recyclable and fully biodegradable.

CANADA SILVER BEAVER BADGE

Participate in our Online Classes to earn these exclusive digital badges!
www.toptenaward.org

Design & Development by:

Tara Asadi

1) Genetic mutations. While _____ has banned DBP from all children's toys, no action has yet been taken against its presence in cosmetics.
A) Mexico
B) Canada
C) USA
D) Germany
ANSWER:

2) Focusing on skincare, Natural ingredients like fruit enzymes, _____ _____ and organic herbs.
A) Vitamin A
B) Vitamin E
C) Vitamin C
D) Vitamin B
ANSWER:

3) Natural and oleochemical ingredients are less unlikely to cause skin irritation or allergic reactions.
A) True
B) False
ANSWER:

3) Correct Sentence: Natural and oleochemical ingredients are less likely to cause skin irritation or allergic reactions.
A) True
B) False
ANSWER:

4) By _____, the organic beauty market will reach 25.11$ billion.
A)2025
B)2020
C)2035
D)2023
ANSWER:

5) While petrochemicals may deliver short-term _____, the long-term effects can be highly toxic to humans and the environment.
A) results
B) effects
C) problems
D) All of Them
ANSWER:

6) Manufacturers shifting to _____ _____ production have a promising future.
A) European Market
B) sustainable cosmetics
C) old fashion
D) All of Them
ANSWER:

7) If you want to branch into the world of sustainable, _____-derived products, begin with some of these safe and effective ingredients.
A) Petrochemical
B) metallic
C) Oleochemical
D) All of Them
ANSWER:

8) Enhances Brand Reputation. _____ _____ send a message to consumers — this company is committed.
A) High Standard
B) European Brand
C) Green products
D) New Model
ANSWER:

9) By choosing sustainable cosmetics, a consumer forgoes the stress and uncertainty of toxic, synthetic products and invests in their long-term _____ and beauty.
A) Health

B) Economy
C) Result
D) New Model
ANSWER:

10) Why Buy Natural and Sustainable Cosmetics. banning the small plastics, illustrating that environmental stewardship is a increasing priority to the nation and its consumers
A) True
B) False
ANSWER:

11) Towards sustainable, _____ _____, you show your global and social awareness.
A) High Standard
B) European Brand
C) Green products
D) New Model
ANSWER:

12) _____ and ____ are synthetic antioxidants used as preservatives, and they are most common in lipsticks and moisturizing creams.
A) Co & Co2
B) BHA & BHT
C) COD & COB
D) Nano & Bio
ANSWER:

13) Manufacturing companies interested in venturing into the _____ _____.
A) High Standard
B) European Brand
C) Green Market
D) New Model
ANSWER:

14) Often found in nail products, DBP is a solvent for dyes.
A) True
B) False
ANSWER:

15) The Asia-Pacific region is an area of particular interest for this market since the region accounted for 41.9 percent of the total oleochemicals market in 2013 for its abundance of raw materials and large consumer base.
A) True
B) False
ANSWER:

16) With an increasing number of consumers and retailers demanding cosmetics with natural or sustainable ingredients, the green cosmetics market has experienced a 15 percent annual growth rate.
A) True
B) False
ANSWER:

17) Often found in nail products, _____ is a solvent for dyes.
A) Co2
B) DBP
C) COD
D) Bio
ANSWER:

18) It's not well understood how _____ _____ in personal care products trigger the rashes, called allergic contact dermatitis.
A) Petrochemical items
B) metallic bonds
C) Oleochemical materials
D) chemical compounds
ANSWER:

19) The term "paraben-free" is meant to let consumers know that the harmful chemicals aren't a part of the _____ _____.
A) Product formula
B) metallic bonds
C) Oleochemical materials
D) chemical compounds
ANSWER:

20) When a beauty product is marked as vegan, it means the same thing a vegan.
A) True
B) False
ANSWER:

21) How to Prevent Cosmetic Allergies? Avoid ingredients in cosmetics and skincare products that are irritating to your skin.
A) True
B) False
ANSWER:

22) They might cause an allergic reaction in certain people, and are more likely to irritate those with.
A) True
B) False
ANSWER:

23) A recent example of pollution and consumer demand is the ban of microbeads. Microbeads are tiny pieces of plastic found in many shower scrubs and exfoliating products.
A) True
B) False
ANSWER:

24) The assessment of whether a product is a ECO friendly cosmetic product has to be made on the basis of a case-by-case assessment, taking into account all characteristics of the products.

A) True
B) False
ANSWER:

25) Non-GMO means a product was produced without genetic engineering and its ingredients are not derived from GMOs.
A) True
B) False
ANSWER:

26) Avoid ingredients in cosmetics and skincare products that are irritating to your skin. Look for labels such as "hypoallergenic", "sensitivity tested", "paraben-free", "phthalate-free", "non-comedogenic" and "fragrance-free".
A) True
B) False
ANSWER:

27) Parabens can act like the hormone estrogen in the body and disrupt the normal function of hormone systems affecting male and female reproductive system functioning, reproductive development, fertility, and birth outcomes.
A) True
B) False
ANSWER:

28) Sodium Lauryl Sulfate (SLS) strips the skin of its natural oils which causes dry skin, irritation, and allergic reactions. It can also be very irritating to the eyes. Inflammatory skin reactions include itchy skin and scalp, eczema, and dermatitis.
A) True
B) False
ANSWER:

CANADA BRONZE BEAVER BADGE

Participate in our Online Classes to earn these exclusive digital badges!
www.toptenaward.org

Design & Development by:

Tara Asadi

Bibliography:

Amberg, N.; Magda, R. Environmental Pollution and Sustainability or the Impact of the Environmentally Conscious Measures of International Cosmetic Companies on Purchasing Organic Cosmetics. Visegrad J. Bioecon. Sustain. Dev. 2018, 1, 23.

Asadi, J., "International Environmental Labelling, Economic Consequencies, Export Magazine, July 2001

Asadi, J. 2008. Mobile Phone as management systems tools, ISO Magazine, Vol.8, No.1

Asadi, J., Eco-Labelling Standards, National Standard Magazine, Sep. 2004.

Barbieux, D.; Padula, A.D. Paths and Challenges of New Technologies: The Case of Nanotechnology-Based Cosmetics Development in Brazil. Adm. Sci. 2018, 8, 16.

Basketter, D.; Corsini, E. Can We Make Cosmetic Contact Allergy History? Cosmetics 2016, 3, 11.

Benitta Christy P & Dr. Kavitha S, "GO-GREEN TEXTILES FOR ENVIRONMENT", Advanced Engineering and Applied Sciences: An International Journal 2014; 4(3): 26-28

Chemical Week, 1999. Europe's Beef Ban Tests Precautionary Principle. (August 11).

Chaudri, S.K.; Jain, N.K. History of Cosmetics. Asian J. Pharm. 2009, 7–9, 164–167.

CHOI, J.P. Brand Extension as Informational Leverage. Review of Eco- nomic Studies, Vol. 65 (1998), pp. 655-669.

Conway, G. 2000. Genetically modified crops: risks and promise.

Corrado, M., (1989), The Greening Consumer in Britain, MORI, London

Corrado, M., (1997), Green Behaviour – Sustainable Trends, Sustainable Lives?, MORI, london, accessed via countries. Manila, Asian Development Bank 33p.

Cosmetics, Perfume, & Hygiene in Ancient Egypt. Available online: https://www.ancient.eu/article/1061/cosmetics-perfume--hygiene-in-ancient-egypt/ (accessed on 4 May 2017).

Deo H T, "Eco friendly textile production", Indian Journal of Fibre & Textile Research Vol.26, March – June 2001,pp.61-73Dawkins, K. 1996. Eco-labeling: consumer's right-to-know or restrictive business practice? Minneapolis, Minn., Institute for Agriculture and Trade Policy.

Di Leva, C. E. 1998. International Environmental Law and Development. Georgetown Interna. Environ. Law Review 10 (2): 502-549.

Guerra, E.; Llompart, M.; Garcia-Jares, C. Analysis of Dyes in Cosmetics: Challenges and Recent Developments. Cosmetics 2018, 5, 47. [CrossRef]

Cosmetics Market by Category (Skin & Sun Care Products, Hair Care Products, Deodorants, Makeup & Color Cosmetics, Fragrances) and by Distribution Channel (General Departmental Store, Supermarkets,

Drug Stores, Brand Outlets)—Global Opportunity Analysis and Industry Forecast, 2014–2022. Available online: https://www.alliedmarketresearch.com/cosmetics-market (accessed on 31 July 2016).

General Introduction to the Chemistry of Dyes. Available online: https://www.ncbi.nlm.nih.gov/books/ NBK385442/ (accessed on 12 December 2010).

Economics and Management 43, 339-359,

Eiderstroem, E. 1997. Eco-labeling: Swedish Style. Forum for Applied Research in Public Policy 141(4).

Elkington, J. and Hailes, J. 1990. The green consumer guide: You can buy products that don't cost the earth. New York, Viking Press. 96p.

EMONS, W. Credence Goods and Fraudulent Experts. RAND Journal of Economics, Vol. 28 (1997), pp. 107-119.

EMONS, W. Credence Goods Monopolists. International Journal of In- dustrial Organization, Vol. 19 (2001), pp. 375-389.

European Union official website: https://ec.europa.eu/info/about-european-commission/contact_en

Feenstra, R.C. "Exact Hedonic Price Indexes," Review of Economics and Statistics 77 (1995): 634-653.

Feenstra, R.C., and J.A. Levinsohn. "Estimating Markups and Market Conduct with Multidimensional Product Attributes," Review of Economic Studies (62 (1995): 19-52.

Forest Stewardship Council: "Principles and criteria for forest stewardship" Document 1.2: <http://www.fscoax.org>

Forsyth, K. 1999. Will consumers pay more for certified wood products? Journal of Forestry 97 (2) : 18-22.

Freeman, A. M III. The Measurement of Environmental and Resource Values. Theory and Methods. Washington D.C.: Resource for the Future, 1993.

Friends of the Earth, 1993. Timber certification and eco-labeling. London, FOE:

Geetha Margret Soundri, "Ecofriendly Antimicrobial Finishing of Textiles Using Natural Extract", Journal of International Academic Research For Multidisciplinary, ISSN: 2320 – 5083, 2014, Vol 2.

Graves, P., J.C. Murdoch, M.A. Thayer, and D. Waldman. "The Robustness of Hedonic Price Estimation: Urban Air Quality," Land Economics 64(1988): 220-233.

Halvorsen, R. and R. Palmquist. "The Interpretation of Dummy Variables in Semiloga-rithmic Equations." American Economic Review 70:474-75 (1980).

Imhoff, Dan, and Grose, Lynda, and Carra, Roberto., "Organic Cotton Exhibit," Mimeo. Simple Life and distributed the Texas Organic Cotton Marketing Cooperative, O'Don-nell, Texas (1996).

Imhoff, Dan. "Growing Pains: Organic Cotton Tests the Fibre of Growers and Manufac-turers Alike," reprinted on Simple Life's web page (simplelife.com), but first printed by Farmer to Farmer, December 1995.

Incomplete Consumer Information in Laboratory Markets. Journal of Environmental labeling.

ISO 14020, ISO 14021,ISO 14024,ISO 14025, International Organization for Standardization.

Kennedy, P.E. "Estimation with Correctly Interpreted Dummy Variables in Semilogarith-mic Equations," American Economic Review 71: 801 (1981).

Kirchho®, S., (2000), Green Business and Blue Angels.

Kraus, Jeff. Lab Technician at the North Carolina School of Textiles.

Labeling Issues, Policies and Practices Worldwide.

Lamport, L. 1998. The cast of (timber) certifiers: who are they? International J. Ecofor-estry 11(4): 118-122.

Large Scale impoverishment of Amazonian forests by logging and fire. 1999.

Lathrop, K.W. and Centner, T.J. 1998. Eco-labeling and ISO 14000: An analysis of US regulatory systems and issues concerning adoption of type II standards. Environmental

Lee, J. et al. 1996. Trade related environmental measures; sizing and comparing impacts.

Lehtonen, Markku. 1997. Criteria in Environmental Labeling: A comparative Analysis on Environmental Criteria in Selected Labeling Schemes. Geneva, UNEP. 148p.

LIEBI, T. Trusting Labels: A Matter of Numbers? Working Paper Uni versity of Bern, No. 0201 (2002).

Lindstrom, T. 1999. Forest Certification: The View from Europe's NIPFs. Journal of Forestry 97(3): 25-31. London

Losey, J.E., Rayor, L.S. & Carter, M.E. 1999. Transgenic pollen harms monarch larvae. Nature 399 20 May): p.214.

Management 22 (2) : 163-172.

Mattoo, A. and H. V. Singh, (1994), Eco-Labelling: Policy Considera-Michaels, R. G., and V. K. Smith. "Market Segmentation And Valuing Amenities With Hedonic Models: The Case Of Hazardous Waste Sites," Journal of Urban Economics, 1990 28(2), 223-242.

Nicholson-Lord, D., (1993) 'Tis the Season to be Green, The Independent, 20 December

Nuttall, N., (1993), Shoppers can cross green products off their lists, The Times, 3 July
OCDE/GD(97)105. Paris, OECD. 81p.

OECD. "Ec-labelling: Actual Effects of Selected Programmes," OCDE/GD (97) 105, 1997, Paris. (available on line at http://www.oecd.org/env/eco/books.htm#trademono)

OECD. 1997a. Case study on eco-labeling schemes. Paris, OECD (30 Dec):

OECD. 1997b. Eco-labeling: Actual Effects of Selected Programs.

Osborne, L. "Market Structure, Hedonic Models, and the Valuation of Environmental Amenities." Unpublished Ph.D. dissertation. North Carolina State University, 1995.

Osborne, L., and V. K. Smith. "Environmental Amenities, Product Differentiation, and market Power," Mimeo, 1997.

Ozanne, L.K. and Vlosky, R.P. 1996. Wood products environmental certification: the United States perspective". Forestry Chronicle 72 (2) : 157-165.

Palmquist, R. B., F. M. Roka, and T.Vukina. "Hog Operations, Environmental Effects, and Residential Property Values," Land Economics 73(1), (1997): 114-24.

Palmquist, R.B. "Hedonic Methods," in J.B Braden and C.D. Kolstad, eds. Measuring the Demand for Environmental Improvement. Amsterdam, NL: Elsevier, 1991.

Pento, T. 1997. Implementation of Public Green Procurement Programs (22-31) in Greener Purchasing: Opportunities and Innovations. Sheffield, Greenleaf Publ. 325 p.

Perloff, J. "Industrial Organization Lecture Notes," Mimeo. University of California at Berkeley (1985).

Plant, C. and Plant, J. 1991. Green business: hope or hoax? Philadelphia, New Society Publishers 136 p.

Polak, J. and Bergholm, K. 1997. Eco-labeling and trade: a cooperative approach (Jan.): Policy in a Green Market. Environmental and Resource Economics 22, 419-

Poore, M.E.D. et al. 1989. No timber without trees. London, Earthscan. 352p.

Raff, D. M.G., and M. Trajtenberg. "Quality-Adjusted Prices for the American Automobile Industry: 1906-1940." NBER Working Paper Series, Working Paper No. 5035, February 1995.

Roberts, J. T. 1998. Emerging global environment standards: prospects and perils. Journal of Developing Societies 14 (1): 144-163.

Rosen, S., "Hedonic Prices and Implicit Markets: Product Differentiation in Pure Competition." Journal of Political Economy. 82: 34-55 (1974).

Ross, B. 1997. Eco-friendly procurement training course for UN HCR. : 126 p.

Ryan, S., and Skipworth, M., (1993), Consumers turn their backs on green revolution, The Times, 4 April

Salzman, J. 1997. Informing the Green Consumer: The Debate over the Use and Abuse of Environmental Labels. Journal of Industrial Ecology 1 (2): 11-22.

Sanders, W. 1997. Environmentally Preferable Purchasing: The US Experience (946-960) in Greener Purchasing: Opportunities and Innovations. Sheffield, Greenleaf Publ. 325p.

Sayre, D. 1996. Inside ISO 14000: The competitive advantage of environmental management. Delray Beach FL., St. Lucie Press. 232p.

SHAPIRO, C. Premiums for High Quality Products as Returns to Reputa- tion. Quarterly Journal of Economics, Vol. 98, No. 4 (1983), pp. 659-680.

Stillwell, M. and van Dyke, B. 1999. An activists handbook on genetically modified organisms and the WTO. Washington DC., The Consumer's Choice Council: 20 p.

Semenzato, A.; Costantini, A.; Meloni, M.; Maramaldi, G.; Meneghin, M.; Baratto, G. Formulating O/W Emulsions with Plant-Based Actives: A Stability Challenge for an Eective Product. Cosmetics 2018, 5, 59.

Teisl, M. F., B. Roe, and R. L. Hicks. "Can Eco-labels tune a market? Evidence from dolphin-safe labeling," Presented paper at the 1997 American Agricultural Economics Association Meetings, Toronto.

THE GERSEN, C. Psychological Determinants of Paying Attention to Eco- Labels in Purchase Decisions: Model Development and Multinational Vali- dation. Journal of Consumer Policy, Vol. 23, No. 4 (2000), pp. 285-313.

Tibor, T. and Feldman, I. 1995. ISO 14000: a guide to the new environmental management standards. Burr Ridge Ill., Irwin Professional Publ. 250 p.

Torre, I. de la, & Batker, D. K. (n.d.) 1999-2000. Prawn to trade: prawn to consume. Graham WA., Industrial Shrimp Action Network (isatorre@seanet.com), [and] Asia –Pacific Townsend, M. 1998. Making things greener: motivations and influences in the greening of manufacturing. Aldershot, England, Ashgate Publisher. 203p.

U.S. Energy Information Administration, What is U.S. Electricity Generation by Energy Source?, Retrieved From: https://www.eia.gov/tools/faqs/faq.php?id=427&t=3

U.S. Energy Information Administration, Biomass Explained, Retrieved From: https://www.eia.gov/energyexplained/?page=biomass_home

U.S. Environmental Protection Agency. National Water Quality Fact Inventory: 1990 Report to Congress. EPA 503-9-92-006, Apr. 1992.

UK Eco-labelling Board website, accessed via http://www.ecosite.co.uk/Ecolabel-UK/

US Environmental Protection Agency (EPA742-R-99-001): 40 p. <www.epa.gov/opptintr/epp>

US EPA, 1993. Determinants of effectiveness for environmental certification and labeling programs. Washington, D.C., US Environmental Protect

US EPA, 1993. Status report on the use of environmental labels worldwide. Washington, D.C., US Environmental Protection Agency (742-R-93-001 September).

US EPA, 1993. The use of life-cycle assessment in environmental labeling. Washington, D.C., US Environmental Protection Agency (742-R-93-003 September).

US EPA, 1998. Environmental labeling: issues, policies, and practices worldwide. Washington DC., Environmental Protection Agency, Pollution Prevention Division Prepared by Abt

US EPA, 1999. Comprehensive procurement guidelines (CPG) program. Washington, D.C., US Environmental Protection Agency: <www.epa.gov/cpg>

US EPA, 1999. Environmentally preferable purchasing program: Private sector pioneers: How companies are incorporating environmentally preferable purchases. Washington, D.C.,

USG, 1993. Federal acquisition, recycling, and waste prevention. Washington DC., Executive Order: (20 October).

USG, 1998. Greening the government through waste prevention, recycling, and federal acquisition. Washington, D.C., Executive Order 13101 (September).

Kijjoa, A.; Sawangwong, P. Drugs and Cosmetics from the Sea. Mar. Drugs 2004, 2, 73–82. [CrossRef]

Wang, J.; Pan, L.; Wu, S.; Lu, L.; Xu, Y.; Zhu, Y.; Guo, M.; Zhuang, S. Recent Advances on Endocrine Disrupting Eects of UV Filters. Int. J. Environ. Res. Public Health 2016, 13, 782.

Bilal, A.I.; Tilahun, Z.; Shimels, T.; Gelan, Y.B.; Osman, E.D. Cosmetics Utilization Practice in Jigjiga Town, Eastern Ethiopia: A Community Based Cross-Sectional Study. Cosmetics 2016, 3, 40.

Ting, C.T.; Hsieh, C.M.; Chang, H.-P.; Chen, H.-S. Environmental Consciousness and Green Customer Behavior: The Moderating Roles of Incentive Mechanisms. Sustainability 2019, 11, 819.

Chen, K.; Deng, T. Research on the Green Purchase Intentions from the Perspective of Product Knowledge. Sustainability 2016, 8, 943.

Wang, H.; Ma, B.; Bai, R. How Does Green Product Knowledge Eectively Promote Green Purchase Intention? Sustainability 2019, 11, 1193.

Nguyen, T.T.H.; Yang, Z.; Nguyen, N.; Johnson, L.W.; Cao, T.K. Greenwash and Green Purchase Intention: The Mediating Role of Green Skepticism. Sustainability 2019, 11, 2653.

Cinelli, P.; Coltelli, M.B.; Signori, F.; Morganti, P.; Lazzeri, A. Cosmetic Packaging to Save the Environment: Future Perspectives. Cosmetics 2019, 6, 26.

Eixarch, H.; Wyness, L.; Siband, M. The Regulation of Personalized Cosmetics in the EU. Cosmetics 2019, 6, 29.

CANADA GOLD BEAVER BADGE

Participate in our Online Classes to earn these exclusive digital badges!

Design & Development by:

Tara Asadi

Environmental Lifestyle Guide

For Grade 9

For Grade 10

Plus Online Certification Tests via:
https://toptenaward.org

Standard Text Books

For Grade 11

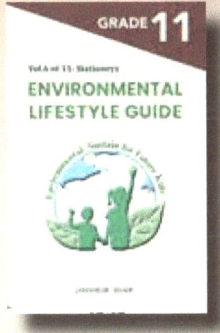

For Grade 12

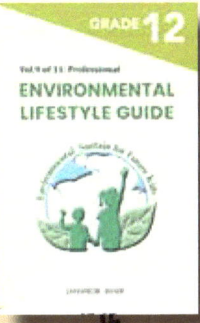

**Environmental Lifestyle Guide
Standard Text Book**
For Students Grade 9 to 12
Available in more than
39,000 Bookstores
all over the globe.
https://ecofriendlyeducation.com

**Cooperation by:
Top Ten Award International Network
&
Environmental Sustain for Future Kids**

www.ingramcontent.com/pod-product-compliance
Lightning Source LLC
Chambersburg PA
CBHW040858120626
46551CB00001B/73

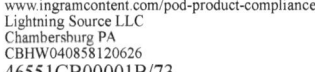